Pause Between
the Years

Pause Between the Years

Insightful Messages Captured in Moments of Self-Reflection, Awakening to What Truly Matters.

MICHELE L. REYNOLDS

ISBN: Paperback 979-8-9887484-0-3
ISBN: E-book 979-8-9887484-1-0

Design and publishing assistance by The Happy Self-Publisher

Dedication

This book is dedicated to All who are willing to go beyond the deeper meaning of life.

Table of Contents

Introduction

Early one morning as I tossed and turned in bed at 4 am, I made a bold decision to write. I felt the need to release my thoughts and emotions, trying to make sense of all that just happened. My husband Mike had just been diagnosed with Multiple Myeloma Cancer. Getting this kind of news completely turned our world upside down. Life as we once saw it no longer exists. My writings first began to follow the journey of my husband's recovery through my eyes as his caregiver and wife, then slowly progressed from observations to a deeper understanding of life, tapping into curiosity and asking the question: "Why"?

I have always been a "why" person. Questioning the meaning of life experiences, whether good or bad, leads me to believe every situation and event we encounter is here to teach us powerful lessons, not only for ourselves, but for others as well. Going through this experience has taught me the importance of appreciating life and learning to **pause between the years** to fully capture the meaningful moments, each and every day.

The book you are now holding in your hands consists of 52 messages, one for each week of the year. A compilation of analogies, inspiration, words of encouragement, genuine authenticity, and empowerment, along with self-reflection and inner healing. Messages of transforming setbacks into powerful self-discoveries, while also reflecting on the elements of nature that surround us, with a touch of profound wisdom sprinkled throughout.

This book creates an awareness of beauty even in the most painful and difficult times, with an understanding that messages often come to us in mysterious ways. It's up to us to recognize the hidden gifts from within.

This book is written with the sole purpose. No matter what message you read; it is my aspiration that these words will be just what you needed at the right exact time creating a powerful transformation from within.

-Michele L. Reynolds

"...gracefully stepping into the unknown."

What is my why...

*E*xpressing my thoughts on paper was a decision I made early one morning. The more I wrote, the better I felt. I realized that healing occurs from within, simply from deciding to release and surrender. My writings started out as stories of hardships, challenges, and grief, then transformed into inspirational messages, inviting curiosity to pause and reflect on life experiences.

I write to inspire and encourage others to recognize their power from within. I write to bring awareness to the simplicity of life and appreciation of all surroundings. I write to share authenticity and vulnerability, and to urge others to gracefully share theirs. I write to ignite the light within you to pursue your "why" and release the fear, gracefully stepping into the unknown, knowing you've been worth it all along.

"...your voice is more powerful than you know."

Finding your voice...

*I*t starts with awareness, followed by a feeling. The realization of your uniqueness comes alive with absolute conviction as you decide to release old habits that no longer serve you. Speak from your heart and give yourself permission to courageously let the words flow out one by one. Your voice is more powerful than you know. It is an expression of oneself that opens the doorway to a better understanding of who you really are. Say what you *want* to say, instead of what you *should* say. There is something so freeing about letting go of fear as you lean into your voice. The world needs to hear the message you have to share. The days of silently sitting on the sidelines are over. Give voice to what you know to be true and watch the power unleash before your eyes.

"...you are the captain of your ship."

A letter to myself...

*T*urn the page of your life. Ahead is the blank sheet, waiting to be filled with beautiful colors.

Let go of the black and white, as you are destined for greatness.

The gift within you is waiting to emerge. Free your soul and keep moving forward, knowing the best is yet to come.

Recognize your strength and the beauty within as you choose to live your dreams, no longer silencing them. The world needs a little of you sprinkled over their lives. Every day is another chance to begin again. Know your worth and allow your light to shine. It will happen when the time is right.

Sometimes you may get lost on your journey. Understand, good things take time. Follow your intuition. Everything you need is already within you. Turn your attention within and embrace who you are today. Your words have power, so change your language and reset your pattern. You are the captain of your ship. Leave behind your fears and doubts and trust that you were born to stand out. Show the world the real you . . . They have been patiently waiting.

"...perfection is fear disguised
as beautiful artwork."

Let go of Perfection...

hy do we feel the need to be perfect? Do we believe deep within our souls that we are not enough? We may feel inadequate at times or judgmental within ourselves, lacking the confidence to move forward, assuming we may not get it just right. We hold ourselves back in fear of failing. These emotions overwhelm us, as they paralyze our bodies. We choose to color inside the lines while running on the hamster wheel, being the observer of life, watching others live their lives. We unknowingly look outside ourselves for our worth and sense of value.

Choosing courage to color outside those lines will end this vicious cycle and allow you to appreciate the imperfections with profound freedom. Empowerment will fill your inner being with gratitude, allowing permission to fall with grace and admiration. Deciding to take a chance on yourself puts you in the game instead of being a spectator. Life is ever changing. Learning to live in the grey areas with an open heart gives you permission to soar.

Perfectionism is fear, disguised as beautiful artwork. Set a new pattern . . . Let go and discover that your imperfect self is more powerful than your perfect silence.

"...we are in constant motion just like the hands on a clock."

Learning to Pause...

*L*ife passes us by in the blink of an eye. If we don't take the time to pause, we will miss out on the most magnificent and meaningful experiences that are right in front of us. Choosing to be consistent with our thoughts and ideas will create a path to become the ultimate version of who we truly are. Learning how to regulate our emotions by awareness skillfully strengthens our internal beliefs. We are in constant motion, just like the hands on a clock, endlessly changing with every second, evolving and growing. We come to understand that the past, present, and future exist simultaneously.

Deciding to elevate yourself empowers your identity to explore unchartered territories with enthusiasm and with curiosity of the road ahead. Rediscover your joy, let go of your fear, and take a soft pause. . . You are worth the wait.

"...surrounding ourselves in this space of green."

Walking in Nature...

Step by step you hear the crackle and crunch of the dried leaves that fall to the ground beneath your feet. As you look left and right, you witness the radiant shades of color amongst the trees along the path. Their slender trunks reach endlessly up to the sky, one by one standing together in unison. The leaves cover the ground, like a warm blanket on a cold night. In the distance you hear rustling in the bushes awakening your curiosity. You proceed further along, only to realize it was a family of squirrels enjoying their day. You feel the warmth of the sun throughout your body, as peace fills the air anticipating your journey ahead. You weave in and out of the trails with curiosity of its destination. Along the way you stumble across pinecones, nestled beneath broken branches that were once tree limbs. The scent of nature is carried through the air in the slight breeze you feel against your skin.

Surrounding ourselves in this space of green creates calmness and tranquility without distractions, while allowing healing to take place as we become mindful of living in the present moment.

"...our words are powerful
tremendous gifts."

Forget your script; say what your heart needs to say...

*W*hat does it truly mean to speak from the heart? For me it has always been a feeling, deep within the core of my being. A yearning for the translation of my message to reach the heart of others. A powerful connection, not visible to the eye. Allowing vulnerability to be released with certainty opens the path of genuine authenticity. Having the ability to move your listener from a deeper place that is so unforgettable.

Your heart holds your life experiences close to your spirit. It's the central wisdom of feeling. Your words are powerful, tremendous gifts. Your words flow subconsciously like that of a river flowing downstream. Sharing your stories in the raw demonstrates a sense of freedom and courage, while inspiring others to do the same. As clarity is revealed, so is the unfolding of miracles.

"...we begin piece by piece building our home from within."

Hardships in life are an opportunity for growth...

*T*here are times in our lives when we experience hardships. The fear felt deep within our core instantly stifles our existence. The overwhelming outburst of tears opens like a floodgate, without resistance. Contemplating our next move seems impossible to comprehend with the surge of emotions being released. The feeling of pain and sorrow acknowledged in our bodies is a signal of suppressed feelings, which we choose to dismiss.

Then, minute by minute, a decision to surrender takes over our soul, releasing the struggle to no longer rebel. We begin piece by piece, building our home from within, stronger than ever before, allowing emotional safety to be reborn. Transforming our power within us to celebrate true liberation becomes our destiny.

Having grace to move forward, while recognizing that the hidden gift within the discomfort was purposely redirecting our path. Trust the hardships and know that bliss is always waiting on the other side.

"...transformation takes place right before your eyes."

Look beyond what you see...

You ou notice a huge stone with its uneven edges as it sits protecting the ground it lays upon, its texture rough and coarse as it stands in isolation from the world. It needs no one as it exists so proudly. The wind and rain cover the outer shell like a blanket as the moisture seeps into the cracks. The sun reflects the layers of marble defining the intricate details etched throughout its surface, exposing glimmers of light. The world around it embraces its strength and uniqueness. Its beauty becomes visible just as it is, and also for what it can become. Imagination then starts to unfold. The corners that were once sharp and pointed, now become soft and smooth. The depth of color seen as dark and grey becomes vibrant with mystical dimensions of hue and brightness. Shape starts to come alive with its curves as it creates pathways of concentrated streams of water, allowing a hypnotic pattern to be heard creating a serene melody with a sense of awe and wonder. Transformation takes place right before your eyes. What once was a piece of marble is now music to your ears.

"...allowing ourselves to soar without limitations."

Beauty of birds...

There is something so beautiful about watching a bird fly across the sky, spreading its wings, fearless of its path ahead. They own the sky without hesitation, roaming the earth as they take in the sites. They fill their lungs with crisp air, while allowing the wind to spread their wings with ease. The sky is the limit as they choose their course of direction. Senses take over, pointing them to a path unknown. They are one with the universe, grounded in the air, free to travel wherever their hearts desire. Opting to fly alone or with a flock is a choice intuitively decided. It's knowing with absolute certainty that moving forward will get them closer to reaching their landing place.

We are all in search of our own destinations. Allowing ourselves to soar without limitations will embody the power of fulfilling one's purpose. All we have to do is spread our wings and fly.

*"...it doesn't have to make sense
to anyone else."*

No longer going against your grain...

C hoosing a path that ignites and fuels your energy is like no other. Creativity starts to seep out of your entire being. It's with you wherever you go, never leaving your side. It grows minute by minute and starts to multiply in every aspect of your life. Ideas and thoughts come alive for the first time with such a profound sense of certainty. The hard shell that was once needed dissolves from your body, exposing your true identity with unconditional love. You know with certainty you are on the right path. The emptiness you once felt is no longer with you. You only feel abundance and anticipation for the days ahead.

You have the right to choose your own path. It doesn't have to make sense to anyone else. If something doesn't feel right and you're not allowing your true authenticity to shine, step back and pause. You simply may just be going against your grain.

"...an illusion due to the fear of the unknown."

False obstacles...

*T*he natural course of becoming is a gift we give ourselves. Patience and acceptance are a constant reflection instilled on our journey. Always knowing that all is well as we connect to our inner guidance, tapping into our intuition. There is an understanding of what our next step is as we trust within the universe. Learning to release these roadblocks within our imagination and understanding they are only an illusion due to fear of the unknown. Shifting our awareness allows us to let go of the uncertainties, to shatter those barriers in front of us, and to allow the walls we built to dissolve. We discover our beliefs to follow our purpose with absolute consciousness.

Being aware of the signs around you guides and lifts your spirits with such determination that you are right where you need to be at this very moment. Your desires are moving into form. Continue this path, alter your beliefs, and when you are fearful, do it anyway.

"...stand in your power of knowing."

Letting go of self-doubts...

Self-doubts are just an illusion . . . greatness is born when you release what no longer is good for you. Overcome your limitations, pause and discover your true self. There are infinite ways to expand our lives. Our mindset and emotional intelligence can be altered and changed to support our true being. When we feel different from others, we may look at ourselves as not being normal or like everyone else. Many have different phases of spiritual awakening. Once we start to take away the shoulds of our lives and instead implement our ideas into reality, it's a feeling of immense power. There is a glow about you because of the energy you are expelling from your body. Be that example of authenticity.

Keep following your curiosity and know you're on the right path. Your actions will encourage others to open their doorway to true bliss. The path is right in front of you. It calls and feeds you, along with inspiration and clarity. Follow the impulse. Yield the realizations of your true destiny. Stand in your power of knowing. Prepare for THERE and HERE will get you THERE.

"...constantly changing and evolving."

Colors of leaves...

*T*he various shades of a leaf have such beauty and uniqueness. Each one displays a character untold. The shapes and sizes, along with the textures seem to change appearance at the exact right time, trusting what's in front of them will support their presence unconditionally. There are no doubts or lack of faith, just a constant flow of evolution excited for the next phase of their lives. The shift of seasons brings limitless boundaries for growth and expansion. This eternal energy within anticipates the new adventures along the way. It knows without a doubt the universe has its back and embraces the road ahead. The transformation of its physical appearance encompasses the home in which it lives. It never looks back to question its path, only forward to welcome the unknown, eager for the next stage of its existence.

Our lives are much like leaves on a tree, constantly changing and evolving, while all along adjusting to our world and embracing the process of life.

"...let go of the not knowing and ease into curiosity."

Everything is on its way...

Just like the river flows in constant motion, so do our lives. It is ever changing and evolving, moving relentlessly like the hands of a clock. Sometimes we lose faith, and our minds start to wander with worry and doubt. We push so hard for that one thing we feel so desperately in need of, in order to survive. Listen for the subtleties of the path of least resistance. Change your frequency and tune in to another channel just as you do with a radio station. What is your receptive mode? What are you tuned into? Current reality is temporary, just like life is linear. Shift your vibration and release the limits that you have created throughout your life. Let go of the not knowing and ease into curiosity. Allow the feeling of being, guide and direct you on a path of pure abundance.

Where you put your attention is where you create your life. Trust your inner guidance and watch your life unfold in magical ways.

"...trust and appreciation are felt
throughout the morning sky."

Such beauty in early rise...

*S*tillness in the air as the birds chirp and sing so quietly as they spread their wings with confidence, trusting in the day to come. Deer traveling together with their family as they graze the earth, consuming their morning feed. Flowers bloom as they stretch and expand their petals as the sun awakens their roots. Trees bloom and continuously grow as they reach out to one another, absorbing the moisture in the air. Sun so effortlessly rising as it surrounds the earth with warmth and brightness like a soft blanket on a brisk night. Animals and insects awaken as they communicate in their own language, hand in hand with one another no matter the distance or space between them. Trust and appreciation are felt throughout the morning sky as nature connects one another without judgment or despair.

Nature provides us with an example of how we can live our lives daily. Taking the time to sit in stillness is where the answers lie to live a simple, peaceful life. Just as the wind is felt but not seen, so is the energy that flows throughout us, connecting us as one within the universe.

"...the art of slowing down and appreciating the simplicity."

Rainy days...

*H*ave you ever watched the rain early in the morning? You hear the pitter patter of the drops as they fall easily to the ground. You witness how the trees sway back and forth as if they are dancing to the rhythm with no resistance. They absorb the water from the tops of their tall branches and allow the natural flow to take over their roots as it falls into the ground and is absorbed throughout the earth. It not only nourishes the trees which can be seen, it also feeds the insects and animals without greed. Nature knows without a doubt that there is plenty to go around and is never concerned about not having enough. It is a belief and faith never disturbed, trusting in the process.

Rain also has a profound effect on people . . . It creates such a calmness in our bodies as we listen to the drops fall to the ground from inside our homes. We gaze out our windows as we observe this natural beauty which somehow hypnotizes us into a state of tranquility. We relax without any effort and look forward to the day, knowing peace and harmony is what our bodies have been yearning for.

The art of slowing down and appreciating the simplicity of what is all around us is a gift that we can access at any time. You just have to look in between the drops and appreciate.

"...guidance from within is felt
unconditionally."

Fulfilling your life's purpose...

E arly in the morning as you open your eyes, you experience a sense of peace and bliss. A surge of adrenaline runs through your body as it takes over your wellbeing. You move about your day with such ease and calmness. Creativity starts to come alive in ways you've never experienced before. Thoughts and ideas run aimlessly throughout your mind like a river flowing downstream. There is no resistance against the current, only trust and appreciation. You begin to trust the process and understand the need to let go of the outcome. Being in the present moment becomes a natural state of mind, rather than a struggle to obtain. There is a sense of knowing with such confidence and commitment that you are right where you need to be. Guidance from within is felt unconditionally, never leaving your side.

There becomes an understanding that we are all born with such beautiful gifts. Choosing to tap into them with certainty and confidence opens a world of endless opportunities. This is where your purpose of life truly begins.

"...it covers the trees like a warm blanket."

Snowfall...

Why are we so mesmerized as we sit watching the snow fall through our windows? It seems to hypnotize us as we focus on each snowflake and watch it effortlessly descend from the sky. It falls when it feels the need to without restriction and hesitation, and profoundly drops to the earth so silently as if not to disturb or frighten anyone in its path. It covers the trees like a warm blanket and provides softness to little kids as they play so joyously in between the crystals so white. It provides happiness and comfort, along with peace and calmness. We often lay in the snow having the urge to make snow angels. Interesting how our minds take us to a place where we feel safe and want to broaden our wings. Our minds become creative without doubt and disappointment. We slide down the mountains with the snow beneath us as if we feel fearless and in complete control. We build snowmen and construct them in a way that brings us happiness. We dress them with huge smiles and dimples and clothe them with scarves and hats to keep them warm. Why does this white substance we call snow have such a profound effect on human beings? Is it because we truly are connected to the universe and nature? I believe we truly are one . . . There is no division, only true bliss when combined.

"...your mind becomes curious where there are no boundaries."

See beauty in the small things...

*B*irds fly so effortlessly throughout the sky with no attachments and restrictions as they spread their wings, while taking in the beauty all around them. They seem to have a sense of certainty, flying fearlessly as they absorb the abundance of air. Often, they flock together in groups, and other times they fly independently. They are never judged or criticized, only seen as unconditional beauty. You become hypnotized by their stillness and curiosity as you observe them perched upon a tiny branch. Your mind becomes curious, wondering what it would be like to be in their world. Such freedom, where there are no boundaries, nor right or wrong, just being.

Discovering beauty in small things makes it possible to discover beauty in everything.

"...no matter what comes our way we
will stand tall."

Trees and human beings...

One day, as I sat looking outside my window, I noticed the magnitude of the wind. The leaves were blowing from left to right. The temperature was declining, and a storm was about to come. I observed the tallness and large trunk of this one particular tree . I imagined the roots scattered beneath the earth, one by one holding on tightly with intense support. I recognized the bravery of this tree as it stood tall. Unaware of what was about to come its way. It seemed to trust the process and knew without a doubt it was going to be okay.

We are not so different than a tree. Throughout our lives, we are hit with unexpected circumstances and just like the tree branches swaying back and forth, we too are moving and weaving in and out, enduring the uncomfortable and sometimes devastating events, only to realize we have a steady trunk that grounds us. Our strength is redefined and assured, and no matter what comes our way, we will stand tall. Just like a tree, which teaches us to go with the flow. We learn to not resist, but to lean in and trust that we are always supported in a way that may not always be visible. Just like the roots that are not seen from a tree, so is our grounding and strength from within.

"...allow ideas to sprout and take form."

Grow your own seeds...

Seeds, so tiny, yet so powerful. They attach themselves to the earth and become one with the universe as they continue to grow. Their strength increases everyday as they mature. Nature hydrates them as their buds start to take shape. The vibrant colors expand as they stretch up to the sky. The minutes and hours progress throughout the morning, nurturing every inch of their being. Insects are drawn to them for comfort and security.

We all have tiny seeds within us, waiting to take root, trusting that growth will come about as time evolves. We recognize the light and rise to the opportunities that lie in front of us. We allow ideas to sprout and take form from the start of imagination. Appreciate the phases of creativity and excitement of what's to come, while all along remembering it all started with just one seed.

"...you are reminded just as they serve a
purpose so do you."

Pebbles on your path...

*D*ay by day you stumble upon pebbles on your path. Sometimes you walk over them unnoticed, other times they catch your attention with a jolt of pain. You soon forget the discomfort and continue on your journey. You learn to build tolerance, as this is all you know. The pebbles become part of your life, leaving marks embedded in your soul. You start to make room for them, anticipating their existence. You tune out the irritation by staying strong on the exterior. You figure the harder the shell, the less impact. Then a shift takes place as your awareness becomes heightened. You learn to look around, no longer avoiding these obstacles, instead embracing them as blessings. You are reminded just as they serve a purpose, so do you. After all, they were never meant to stop you, only slow you down a bit.

"...let go of things that no longer serve you."

Lean into you...

*A*llow space for yourself, as you take ownership of your worthiness. Wipe your tears with compassion as you would for a loved one. Mend your broken heart with gratitude and appreciation as you stand on your own. Smile at your reflection as you honor your uniqueness. Sit in stillness as you embody the gifts you've been graciously blessed with. Be attentive to your needs as you would for a best friend. Empower yourself as you choose courage over fear. Permit your emotions to surface through discomfort as you speak from your heart. Let go of things that no longer serve you, as you make room for alignment. Once you embrace the lean . . . the difficultly will then become the extraordinary.

"...have faith and understand that everything is always in the process of working out."

Allow things to fall into place...

One morning as I awoke, I noticed a necklace sitting on my dresser. It was tangled very severely with a bracelet. I would often bypass this necklace, thinking it would be impossible to detach due to the severity of the enmeshed metal.. Days and days went by as it lay, and I wondered if it would miraculously unweave itself. In the past, I would ask my husband to detangle it for me as if he had this magical power. No matter how intertwined they were, he would always be successful in separating them without harm. Then I said to myself, let me try and mimic his actions. So, I grabbed the necklace without force and applied gentle movements as I had witnessed my husband do so many times in the past. As a result, I detached the necklace and bracelet without harm.

I realized many times we go through life having to force things to happen. We may put too much pressure and stress on the situation when it's not necessary. We run from what we refer to as "issues," when in reality it's often an opportunity to solve a problem. Have faith and understand that everything is always in the process of working out. Once we stop resisting, we allow things to unravel as they should, just like that precious metal. Then and only then, things will fall into place as they were meant to.

"...we can choose how we move forward."

Aging is beautiful...

～～～

When we think of age, we often fear it. Our bodies go through changes that some would call less desirable. We begin to see wrinkles and creases around our eyes that once were not there. Grey appears randomly throughout our vibrant-colored hair. We may start to forget things and feel that our minds are not as sharp as they used to be.

What if we could change the narrative and view aging as a timeless beauty with lots of wisdom. The wrinkles and creases around your eyes are there because of all of the laughter that you experienced. The greyness in your hair is a true testimony that you are living life to its fullest. The forgetfulness we may often experience is a true indication to slow down and appreciate our brilliant minds and allow ourselves grace.

Aging is an acceptance and true understanding of who we are with profound admiration of oneself. We can choose how we move forward, appreciate the years we have lived, and the years that are yet to come.

"...every gift has an impact."

People are gifts to us...

Beautiful souls come into our lives at the exact right time. Some are wrapped in magnificent paper and exquisite bows, while others are in a small plain box. We may judge them purely by their appearance, assuming the fancier the better, while ignoring the simple ones that get overlooked. We believe the more gifts we have the better. We sometimes seem to forget that behind the gifts are words unspoken, transmitting kindness to one another. It is invisible to the eye, yet so powerful. The smallest gifts are quite often the most meaningful.

Becoming aware and deciding to share our own gifts inspires, motivates, and encourages others to do the same. Every gift has an impact, but no one benefits if we're not willing to go first. All we need to do is recognize, acknowledge, and share, as I have done right now with you.

"...abundance is not something we acquire, it's something innately we already have."

There is an abundance all around us...

There are times we gaze up at the sky in the evening, witnessing a multitude of stars, millions of them aimlessly scattered throughout the atmosphere. Our minds start to envision different shapes as we connect them one by one. Bright sunny days may bring a mixture of clouds rolling by reflecting back to us our deepest thoughts projected on a screen. The blades of grass beneath our feet run rapidly across the earth, creating a cushion felt so softly between our toes. The sounds and sights of the ocean provide calmness and tranquility as we watch the waves roll in and out one by one with no end in sight.

We often come from a place of scarcity that produces fear of never having enough. Being able to observe life just as it is creates an appreciation for our presence and what we already have. Abundance is not something we acquire, it's something we innately already have.

"...love who you've been, but also love
who you're becoming."

Butterfly moments...

We often admire the beauty of a butterfly but forget the transformation that took place before it spread its wings. These wonderful creatures fly so gracefully, touching the earth, reminding us that change is possible. Experiencing moments of darkness and despair are opportunities for growth, understanding they are temporary, just like a caterpillar leaving its cocoon and trusting the best is yet to come. Moments in life can alter your trajectory in the most significant way. Being faced with situations that may feel hopeless somehow transforms us, providing strength and courage to move forward. We too can leave our dark places of isolation and spread our wings, allowing our souls to shine. Love who you've been, but also love who you're becoming, knowing it's never too late to unfold your wings and fly.

"...our power comes from within."

Every observation is a
teaching moment...

*O*ne morning as I looked out our patio door, I noticed a baby bird had fallen from its nest. I observed as it chirped loudly trying to get its mother's attention. It continued for hours, never giving up. As the hours passed, the baby bird gasped for air frantically in hopes his mother would soon return. Sadly, she was nowhere in sight. The next morning came and I witnessed the bird laying rigid and still. The energy within him had dissipated and was no more. The chirping and subtle movements had vanished before my eyes.

In that instant, I realized our physical bodies are merely shells of our life force. Our power comes from within, allowing energy and connection with others. It flows through us, providing strength and support, connecting our inner harmony.

Reflecting on the baby bird lying so still and lifeless reminded me that the true essence of life goes beyond our physical bodies. We realize how precious we are, even greater than our eyes can see.

"...go with the flow and embrace the moments."

Just a walk in the park...

*N*ature has a way of teaching us the simplicity of life, mirroring back to us what our eyes need to see at the exact right time. Walking in the park, observing the roots intertwined with one another simplifies unity and connection. The patches of grass that multiply as the seasons change, represent nurturing and growth. The kids playing with one another joyfully remind us not to take life so seriously. The birds singing in harmony, flying aimlessly throughout the sky, symbolize freedom and expansion.

The meaningful things in life are not only seen, but also felt.. Life is an experiment waiting to be discovered. Having the courage to break the mold that has kept you stifled will change the trajectory of your future. Go with the flow and embrace the moments, as you immerse yourself in the present. Life was not meant to be a struggle, just a walk in the park.

"...become your biggest champion with unconditional love."

I approve of myself...

Sometimes we go through life seeking approval from others. We feel the need for validation and believe we are not worthy of our decisions. We start to second guess our thoughts, not trusting our own instincts, constantly dismissing ourselves. We unintentionally give our power to others, permitting them to take the driver's seat while we quietly sit in the back observing. We begin to understand that seeking approval holds us back from our true self.

Deciding to take the reins back places the power back in our hands. We become aware of our own feelings and values. Staying true to who we are provides strength to release the attachments outside of ourselves. Understanding the motive behind needing approval is the first step to change. Once we realize the only person we need approval from is ourselves . . . the world becomes a playground with unlimited potential. Become your biggest champion with unconditional love, understanding it's not the job of others to approve of you, it's yours.

"...believing your destination has already arrived."

Becoming...

*T*houghts turn into things as you explore your creativity and discover unlimited possibilities. The unfolding of your destination is felt with profound freedom. It's the little moments along the way that must be savored. Your eyes start to recognize the gifts along the way that may have gone unnoticed in the past. Your hearing becomes heightened with the harmony of nature in its simplicity, like music to our ears. Your heart is at the helm, navigating your path with love and compassion, offering your gifts to the world. Happiness and joy are bursting throughout your existence, enjoying the walk instead of the run.

Allowing yourself to slow down is the recipe for appreciation and gratitude, believing your destination has already arrived. You no longer resist, but embrace, letting go of the outcome, knowing the becoming is what truly matters.

"...it speaks loudly through the quietness."

Inner voice...

*W*hen you choose to be silent, you shed light on your inner voice, allowing it to present itself fully without hesitation. Giving it permission to be your guide as it knows the path ahead. It speaks loudly through the quietness, appreciating space with absolute clarity. It's the internal dialogue undisturbed, directing you to your higher self.

Listening to the soft whispers that offer insight and direction will be your compass to a peaceful and joyful life. Deciding to turn inward allows you to hear your innate intelligence, rather than outside yourself. Removing the fear and doubt as you invite your inner wisdom to show up, reveals answers that you have been longing for. Always remember the voice that is often the quietest, is the one worth listening to.

"...deciding to embrace this power
and allowing it to shine."

Light comes in different forms...

You gaze at the sky in the evening, mesmerized by the multitude of stars that light up the universe. You notice a full moon and see the expansion of illumination as you observe beauty in its true bliss. You wake in the early hours and catch a glimpse of the sun rising as it creates a glow of warmth and beauty with hues of the rainbow.

You take a walk in the park, greeted by a beautiful smile from a stranger. You come across another who gives a slight nod and one with more of a gentle smile. As you walk into a convenience store, someone patiently holds the door open for you without hesitation. These are true examples of light. They come in many shapes and forms around us at all times. However, they may go unnoticed. They warm our hearts, lift our spirits, and connect with us so deeply. We all carry this aura of light within us. Deciding to embrace this power and allowing it to shine, gives permission for others to luminate theirs.

"...let go of the rigidness of who you think you are so you may become come all that you are."

Let go of your labels...

We go through life often attaching ourselves to titles, not realizing the impact it has on our perception. Believing this is all we will ever be stifles our true potential. These labels are an accumulation of life experiences placed securely in a box, allowing no room for growth. You recognize expansion and freedom when you decide to peel away the layers you have branded allowing your true essence to shine.

Let go of the rigidness of who you think you are, so that you may become all that you are. Learn to appreciate that your labels have all served a purpose along your journey. Having the courage to think outside the box will alter how we package ourselves. Release these limitations of your mind and understand the powerful diverse person you are with unlimited potential. Allowing your labels to dissolve one by one as you move through life will reveal your core essence, permitting the flexibility of your individual uniqueness to shine. Always remember, under those labels are a powerful version of you just waiting to emerge.

"...believing that greatness lies within."

Reach for the stars...

*T*houghts are like stars in the sky, shining so brightly, grabbing our attention as they illuminate their surroundings with unforgettable images. Slowly, pictures start to emerge as the mind expands and connects the dots one by one. Emotions rise to the surface as anticipation builds, releasing bits and pieces of an untold story. These beams of light, majestic and untouchable, navigate our path and symbolize unlimited possibilities with no end in sight.

Capturing these moments that move us in time while channeling our ideas allows for the impossible to emerge. Believing that greatness lies within gives us the ability to overcome obstacles while pursuing our dreams.

Remember you have the power and resilience to transform the world one thought at a time as you allow your vision to surface. Climbing the ladder as you reach the stars will elevate your life to the next level, while always knowing you are way bigger than you appear.

...shed our dry brittle branches, leaving room for new blossoms to appear."

Spring forward...

Walking down your path, you feel a warm gentle breeze covering your body as the sun illuminates your skin. You notice buds appearing sporadically as they awaken, expanding one petal at a time. Trees come alive, replacing their once naked limbs like a coat of armor, providing shade in the midafternoons as you intently sit, reading your favorite novel. The world around you becomes vivid and alive, filled with transformation from one phase to the next. Abundance is awakening, bringing back to life what once was dormant. Energy is heightened as the days are long, absorbing the regeneration of existence.

Just like nature is open to receive, so can we. It's about fertilizing the roots within us and watering our souls while providing a safe place for our hearts to expand. Our world is constantly chirping as a reminder to intently listen to our intuition. Trusting in the universe will allow us to shed our dry brittle branches, leaving room for new blossoms to appear. Leap into spring as you feel inspired and excited, recreating your life one season at a time.

"...we begin to trust in a plan way greater than our own."

Surrender...

Sometimes we go through life faced with situations that overwhelm our entire being, bringing us to our knees. We fight along the way, rejecting and pushing the inevitable, wearing blinders and hoping it will disappear like a bad nightmare. We struggle as our minds race to search for answers through uncertainty and doubt. Once we decide to let go of the battle, we feel a sense of calmness within.

Surrender happens when we accept the absolute of not knowing, and gracefully walk into the eye of the storm with our head held high. We begin to trust in a plan way greater than our own. It's a mental shift easing into what is, rather than what we feel should be.

Embracing the truth while releasing your grip invites synchronicity to unfold in magical ways. It's the divine force letting you know peace and serenity are but moments away.

*"...the gift of wonder is within
all of us."*

Behind the "why" ...

Having a mind full of curiosity fuels the energy within. Your imagination wonders as it investigates the unknown. You dig deep into the comprehension of all matters. It's having the ability to look beyond what's in front of you, understanding there is more than meets the eye. It's a hunger within your soul for clarity and purpose, feeding your mind as you receive the answers, only to desire a thirst for more. It provides insight as it opens up channels for connection and a better understanding of the world we live in, instinctively seeing what most people can't.

The gift of wonder is within all of us. Listening to your own questions is like listening to your heart. It's that internal voice urging you through guidance to explore, with the understanding that there is no need to rush for the answers, only the desire to acquire for more.

...allowing and acknowledging your present experience instead of your life situation."

Acceptance...

*W*e spend our whole lives searching for meaning, so when things don't go as planned, we feel there has been an injustice. We focus on resisting rather than allowing, not realizing a simple shift of our perception can profoundly alter the outcome. Let go of the expectation of fairness and instead look for the lessons behind every challenge. Pure acceptance is where you find peace. Learning to rise up from adversity in the darkest hours is where resilience is born. It's about allowing and acknowledging your present experience instead of your life situation. Choose where you focus your attention and tune into the good. There is purpose in the acceptance of what is. It's about extracting all that is good and releasing it into the world as lessons shared with others.

"...allow the feelings of your experience to be your navigator."

Go with the flow of life...

A s I reflect on a crystalline body of water, I observe hints of blue and green bursting through the waves as it flows with the tide, covering the sand while creating a velvety surface that glistens from the reflection of the sun. Clouds roll by ever so quietly, coming and going with the wind at the helm. I bask in the sun, absorbing the rays as I soak up the atmosphere, captivated by the golden eye in the sky. As the night falls, my eye catches the light of the moon, pulling emotions to the surface as it awakens energy within, illuminating the path ahead.

There are natural rhythms all around you. Key into the sights and sounds as you grab ahold of the magic allowing you to flow with trust. Release yourself from the web of anxiety as you sit in silence, inhaling the abundance of air surrounding your entire being. Allow the feelings of your experience to be your navigator and believe the path you're on was designed specifically for you. As you invite stability, growth and expansion will sprout in all directions, flowing you to the meaning of life.

"...there is never a completion of a task,
only a transition to the next."

Let go of your "To Do" list...

The term "time is of the essence" is used quite often. It is said when something needs to be done immediately. We seem to hurry through activities and chores for absolute completion, as we race the clock, only to have it repeat itself the very next day. We somehow feel once we complete these tasks, only then we can enjoy our lives. What if we had it all wrong. What if instead we embrace our "not to do list?" Choosing not to stress over the little things, choosing not to allow the day to go by without laughing, choosing not to stay indoors, but instead walk in the sunshine and breathe in the fresh air.

We come to understand there is never a completion of a task, only a transition to the next. We must choose to savor the joy and happiness that are discovered in little moments that are not planned or on a list. Life is about thriving, not just existing. One day goes into the next and it's up to us to change our list and intentionally do the things that are ultimately worth living..

"...it propels you forward with a
drive so fierce."

Following your intuition...

～～～

I t starts with a feeling, often followed by a nudge. It's your internal voice quietly whispering nuggets of truth as it connects to your senses, creating an image right before your eyes. It propels you forward with a drive so fierce, never leaving your side, always having your best interest in mind. Recognizing something so powerful without reasoning appears frequently as it captures your attention spontaneously, without thought. Allowing this energy to move through you permits your body to speak its mind.

While there are no road maps for our lives, let your intuition be your inner compass as you access its guidance. Embrace this gift as you shine light on your inner wisdom, exposing your true self. Be patient as you reflect with questioning, "What is this trying to tell me?" Understand the answers will come; they are already within you. All you have to do is listen.

"...clear the path between your head and your heart."

Believe in yourself....

You've been given an amazing gift; thus, it's remained unopened, wrapped so tightly for many years, hidden beneath the layers of life. You dare not open it as you fear what lies inside. Doubts and insecurities take over as you contemplate the unknown and decide its safer enclosed than exposed. Day by day you carry this gift, holding in your mind's eye what could possibly be inside. You ponder, feeling your inner strength bursting, no longer waiting to receive, but more importantly understanding it's your own gift to believe.

Clear the path between your head and heart, overcoming self-doubt, fear, and worry as you become your best friend with absolute clarity, knowing you were always meant for more. Have the courage to expose your true self as you recognize your abilities and gifts that others may not, while holding the highest vision and always embracing you truly are what you believe.

"...there isn't anything you need to do
or say or be, you already are."

Uniqueness within you...

*E*very day we strive to be unique as we present ourselves to the world, always seeking what that individuality is. We rack our brains trying to answer this question, constantly searching outside ourselves. Low and behold we realize it's been staring back at us in the mirror. "YOU" bring that uniqueness in every interaction you have, recognizing you are the only one in the world like you. Realize that your values and life experiences shape the person you're becoming, while embracing your character as it was made specifically for you. Your unique self is the most powerful expression of authenticity. Accept your imperfections in the pursuit of greater self-expression. Embracing those idiosyncrasies and flaws allows for your creativity to come alive. There isn't anything you need to do or say or be, you already are. You are one of a kind. Just like flowers bloom and trees grow, each with their own beauty and meaning, so are you, radiating transparency and awakening your own internal being.

...permitting ourselves to clear our minds as we tune into others speaks volumes."

The art of listening...

Something so simple, yet so powerful is often overlooked during a conversation. One's own voice takes precedent, absorbed in our own internal thoughts, focused only on our next sentence, leaving no room for another to utter a word. This inadvertently sends a message of unimportance to another. Permitting ourselves to clear our minds as we tune into others speaks volumes, letting them know they matter. Providing space and silence opens the vessel for others to freely communicate with ease. An immense feeling of love and support fills the room, listening to the words flow out, nonexistent of time. Emotions become heightened, allowing vulnerability to emerge, knowing they are more than worthy of being heard.

Allowing ourselves to be in the present moment without the need to respond leads us to the art of listening with our eyes, ears, and heart.

"...it mirrors back to us our unique individuality."

Beauty in its natural state...

*A*s we immerse ourselves in nature, our minds begin to open to all possibilities. We let go of the structures we built around us and allow flow into our lives. We start to discover the most intricate details never recognized before. Trees that once blended into the earth are now seen in their uniqueness, standing tall, vivid in color, displaying various shades of green. Tiny blades of grass below our feet once taken for granted are now seen as a sea of emerald, soft and subtle and carrying us throughout our day with ease. Flowers that were once dull in color reserved in the ground are now seen dancing to the rhythm of life, engaging our senses, immersed with appreciation of their originality. Birds chirping simultaneously, once heard as noise, are now music to our ears, creating a beautiful melody.

Appreciating the wonders of nature undisturbed teaches us to admire the awe in ourselves in our most natural state. It mirrors back to us our unique individuality, embracing our true essence at its core while realizing it's not always what we look at, but rather what we see.

"...once you decide to change the way you look at things, everything begins to change."

Moving from fear to freedom...

A heavy weight attached to your body pulls you down relentlessly, as it bears the burden of pain, depleting your energy, keeping you stifled and afraid to move. The world around you is perceived as untrustworthy and not safe, always anticipating that the worst is about to happen. The adrenaline in your body runs rapidly, wanting a place to escape but finding nowhere to go. You feel nudges of pain and discomfort as your internal being cries out for attention, wanting permission to break free from the chains of self-doubt and misbeliefs. Then low and behold a profound shift takes over your body as you self-reflect, questioning your own internal existence. You begin to realize your perception is based on fear, consistently avoiding situations in life, impacting your ability to move forward. Once you decide to change the way you look at things, everything begins to change. You no longer resist what can't be seen, but rather accept what can. Letting go becomes natural and at ease without apprehension, only eagerness with courage and grace. Learning to make peace with uncertainty is the key to unlocking your fear, leading you to a life of absolute and profound freedom.

...our words reflect our internal being, right or wrong, they are ours to own."

Authenticity...

*W*e seem to go about our days weaving in and out of conversations, having the need to say the right things at the right time. Self-judgment and unworthiness rise to the surface, as we shy away from confrontation feeling the need for acceptance from others. Our hearts yearn to speak from within, sharing words unscripted, flowing consciously without hesitation. Allowing ourselves to reveal our true essence at its core opens the path for others to bare their souls releasing parts of them hidden so secretly. Choosing to let go of what others may think opens the connection to your inner voice, giving permission to be revealed from the inside out.

Uncovering our authentic self can be liberating and bonding amongst each other once we choose to love ourselves completely. Our words reflect our internal being, right or wrong, they are ours to own. Once we give ourselves the space to speak our truth unconditionally without reservation, then and only then will we begin to create the life we want with purpose and meaning, no longer compromising who we are, but instead embracing who we are.

"...spread your wings as far as the eye can see between the obstacles you encounter."

Between...

Walk with your head held high between the breaths that are taken. Plant your feet firmly on the ground between the uncertainty and confusion. Spread your wings as far as the eye can see between the obstacles you encounter. Grant yourself space between the chaos of your mind. Create awareness of your internal strength between fear and doubt. Allow uneasiness to be felt between the process of change. Seek for the quietness between the rumbling of the storm. Sense the energy between the words spoken with a friend. Admire your loved one between the breaths that are taken while sleeping. Appreciate the power of touch between times of despair.

Recognizing the "between" moments of life is when transformation takes place. All you have to do is look between the lines.

"...the day has come to show the
world who you truly are."

Unlock "you" ...

Release yourself from the web of anxiety as you sit in silence, inhaling the abundance of air surrounding your entire body. Let go of the burden of life experiences that are less desirable and replace them with gratitude and appreciation of the present moment. Radiate your energy as you shine your inner light, unveiling your true potential as nature's gift.

The day has come to show the world who you truly are, no longer hiding in the shadows of the dark. The uniqueness of your profound existence has been bursting at the seams, eager to soar freely unleashing the best version of your ideal self. Your journey has exposed bits and pieces of your passion through subtle hints, creating a trail for your future.

Acknowledging opportunities as they arise guides you closer to discovering your natural abilities while embracing your most authentic self, finally unlocking the person you were truly meant to be.

Acknowledgments

I would first like to thank my husband, Mike. You are my strength, support and foundation. Thank you for the countless nights you spent listening to me read my writings, over and over again, while always believing wholeheartedly in me and my vision for this book. Your profound courage and determination through your journey of cancer inspired me to dig deep within, searching for a better understanding of life while realizing this as an opportunity to help others. You are truly my everything.

Thank you to my amazing kids, Michael, Anthony and Nicole for your relentless strength and optimism during these past difficult years. You inspired me to step out of my comfort zone, take ownership and embrace life which opened the pathway to writing my book.

To my Mother, Father, siblings Maryann, Marie and Michael, extended family and friends, thank you for your endless support, believing in me and being my biggest cheerleaders every step of the way.

A special thanks to Lois Hoffman (The Happy Self-Publisher) for believing in my idea and guiding me to stay true to my unique voice to bravely share with the world.

About the Author

M ichele L. Reynolds has always been very intuitive by nature. Ever since she was little, she would often ask the question "why?" She was always curious of her surroundings and wanting a deeper understanding of life. As time went on, she became very intrigued by quotes, realizing the powerful effect they had on the mind and emotions. Michele would often create these quotes to share as icebreakers for further engagement and brainstorming sessions during team meetings with her employees at the electrical contracting company she and her husband have owned and operated for over 25 years. Her thirst and desire to gain a better understanding of people and the world around her continued throughout the years. When her husband Mike was diagnosed with Multiple Myeloma Cancer over three years ago, Michele chose writing as an outlet to release her emotions for inner healing. Her writings started as stories of grief and hardships, then transformed into inspirational messages spoken from the heart. For Michele, writing has allowed her the opportunity to shed light on the inner gifts that we all possess, while recognizing beauty even in the most difficult times, gaining an appreciation for life just as it is.

Michele spends much of her time every morning feeding her soul. Whether this is through writing, exercising, meditating, or listening to music or podcasts. Her consistency, passion, and resilience are what drives her purpose. But it's her loyalty, dedication, and perseverance to make a positive impact on the lives of others, that fuels her existence.

You can contact her at painfullybeautifullife.com and/or micheler@painfullybeautifullife.com. Reviews are greatly appreciated wherever you purchased this book.